Jane Curran's *Indiana Girl*, a memoir in verse, celebrates a farm family and their land. Curran's heart tells the stories of parents and grandparents. Her soul describes the world of her youth, "derelict cornstalks silvered in frost," "the sun a red rim, a fox's full moon shadow etched on old snow." "The North Field" demonstrates how deeply the farm occupies Curran's being.

Anne Waters Green, poet and author of *The Season Lengthens*

What Curran calls her "inner landscape" welcomes the reader of *Indiana Girl*. This new collection of poems offers both moments and threads that ask the reader to pause and enjoy a scene or reflect on echoes from surrounding poems. As Curran says, "facts alone can't carry the story." The voice of these poems invites us to trust and, in that trust, to share the world of her "life's geography." Curran joins many other Midwestern writers who seek to define the core of their personal peace through a language that allows them to go home.

A. Carl Bredahl, Emeritus Professor, University of Florida, University of Florida

Through memory, Curran explores her sense of home, its inner landscape, shaped by family, time and the geography of an Indiana farm. There is history here. Lineage. Memories of a life long abandoned and reclaimed through this collection of poems. Whispers of Frost lie buried in her words, and Dickey's bold voice as well.

Bob Mustin, novelist, poet, editor, publisher

Jane Curran's crisp, understated portraits of people and place explore Wolfe's familiar maxim —"You can't go home again." But how often by circumstance we are forced to try. After her father's death and her mother's oncoming dementia, Curran seeks a re-connection to homeplace, but as her moving poems in *Indiana Girl* show, it is a yearning that mere nostalgia can't satisfy. Settling in with her familial and literary namesakes, Curran shares scenes of intimate reflection and nearly-forgotten tragedy, rendered with inventive precision: "starlight, sharp as a butcher's blade, cuts clean edges of shadow and ice." While these fine poems acknowledge the inevitable changes in interior and exterior landscapes — "I know stories of wandering without an arrival"— Curran appreciates that "life, known and settled, would go on."

Kenneth Chamlee, Professor Emeritus of English, Brevard College, author of *Absolute Faith* and *Logic of the Lost*

With finely tuned sensitivity to language and the feelings of the people she writes about, Curran conveys love for her Indiana home along with other realms of human experience.

Richard Graham Professor Emeritus, Franklin College of Indiana.

Indiana Girl is a love song to goodness and the ground from which Curran sprang. The book offers a haunting remembrance of home – a place and a past where readers can hear and smell corn, stroll past Angus cows, recall the horrors of World War II and Vietnam. Filled with vivid detail and epic in scope, the poems honor one's place on the planet until, as the poet writes, "the hawk and the land and I were one."

Especially vivid are the "Histories," snapshots of people with whom Curran grew up. The collection's lyrical language, sweep of time, and tussle with loss make *Indiana Girl* rich and unforgettable.

Karen Luke Jackson, Ed.D., writer, spiritual companion, and Courage & Renewal® retreat leader.

Indiana Girl

Indiana Girl

Poems

by

Jane Mary Curran

Copyright © 2019 Jane Mary Curran

ISBN: 978-1-68454-752-4

Library of Congress No. 2018965554

All rights reserved. No part of this book may be produced or transmitted in any form, or by any means, electronic or mechanical, including photocopying, or by any information storage system, without permission in writing from the publisher or author.

First published by *Gridley Fires Books*,
3/15/2019

Cover design by Lacey O'Connor
Interior art by Lucy Teague

for my family

Contents

Introduction	i
Once a Place	1
Every Land Has its Ghosts	2
In 1936 Grandfather John Brewer Curran	3
Hollyhocks	5
The Great Uncle	6
The North Field	7
War	8
Pearl Harbor	9
Earth and Air	10
In the Dark	11
Where Do You Go?	12
Wagon Train	13
First Day	14
Sleeping Warm on the Farm	15
Reading Charlotte Bronte	16
Scent	18
In Summer	19
October Primitive	20
Red Hats	21
Reading Emily Dickinson	23
Four Moons	25
Reading Doctor Zhivago	26

Contents (Continued)

Histories i	28
Histories ii	29
Histories iii	30
Histories iv	31
Histories v	32
Histories vi	33
Histories vii	34
The Portal	35
Return	36
Histories viii	37
At Ninety-one	38
Season of Dreams	39
by the South Field	40
Reading Thomas Wolfe	41
Once a Place	43

Introduction

When I say home, there is only one place. The farm.
My inner landscape,
my life's geography,
my character,
my self.

In 2007 the double lightning strike of my dad's death and Mother's deepening dementia snapped me back to Orange Township, Rush County, Indiana, the place I'd left behind in 1966 when I went to college.

Suddenly I had to deal with Indiana hospitals, Indiana nursing homes, Indiana doctors, Indiana lawyers, Indiana banks, Indiana funeral homes, Indiana realtors and Indiana goodness. And things began to feel like home.

Floods of memories rolled over me—growing up on the farm, how the ground looked, plowed and ready for planting, best friends from school.

Family long dead came alive in my memory, clearer than they had for decades. Like the prodigal I'd gone a long way away and lived in distant countries for 41 years, but now I had to come back to where my life began. Unlike the prodigal I had no father or elder brother to get a feast going. Instead I had Hoosiers.

In my season of grief I wanted to spend time on the farm. I began to imagine I might move back, refurbish the farmhouse, grow a garden, get a horse. Or two. I walked the farm, reacquainted myself with the woods, crops, the barn now home to a family of foxes. My dad died in a nursing home. I imagined that when Mother came to her dying time, I'd bring her to the farm so she could die at home.

After a couple of years the cold light of reality began to expose my dreams for the dreams they were. I saw I was trying to live my parents' lives in order to keep them alive. I wanted to be another generation on the farm. As long as I drove the same county roads, walked the same fields, as long as I was where we'd lived together, I could imagine I was home. As reality continued to shine its harsh spotlight I saw I could not step into my parents' lives. Too much was different. I had changed. My childhood on the farm, my life in Indiana was past, just as the years my family owned the land were passing moments to a piece of earth that had its own history, its own time. My family were stewards, not owners. I could not stay.

All the poems happened, in memory
if not exactly where or when.
Facts alone can't carry the story.
Facts fall short of love.

I live with the power of memories,
the pull of place,
the landscape of a farm.
In the marrow of my bones,
I'm an Indiana girl.

Once a Place

The Farm
where time flowed backward to how life used to be.

Old ways, old pride, the smokehouse, slatted corn cribs,
an outhouse, a spring in the woods where Black Angus drank
and I found arrowheads close to the ditch.
A hay mow with kittens, an ornery cow with her calf.
Gas lights lit the evenings and tiled stoves heated each room.

I slept under Grandmother's old cotton quilt
and fell asleep listening to rain rap the tin roof.

I was born into time when the home place turned mythic,
when my family sought the safe and familiar,
where life, known and settled, would go on.

Every Land has its Ghosts

Alone I watch the sky turn black.
Starlight, sharp as a butcher's blade,
cuts clean edges of shadow and ice.

Smoke and flames of silent fires,
pale flickers rise in darkness.
Fog, breath of long ago people,
drifts among thickets and rolling lands,
settles into hollows
filled with snows of distant winters
under stars.

In 1936 Grandfather John Brewer Curran

took all he had and purchased the farm.

The family called him Pop,
alive to me only in pictures and stories,
in his absence more powerful than presence.
Less man than legend.

He would have loved you.

In one fading photo Pop stands by the shed,
a handsome old man, slight and straight
in a wide straw hat with his big dog, Bo.
In another he plows the west field behind Belgians.
Pop preferred his horses to engines.

In our house his pipes were lined in their rack,
the wood smoothed by his hand, bowls still rich
with the scent of smoke.
His bookcase held *Look Homeward, Angel*,
The Magnificent Ambersons and *Joseph in Egypt*.

I peered through a pinhole to an empty place,
to sketches where I colored him in.
His pocket watch in a dresser drawer,
his old tools down in the barn.

I'm older now than Pop when he died.
I still look back for a glimpse of him.
I have questions for him and stories to tell.

He would have been so proud of you.

Hollyhocks

nod in the dusky air
by the old smoke house
where the fence used to be.
Their stalks bend with the weight of flowers
like the backs of old women
bent over a hoe.

A warm wind stirs and
my grandmother stands
where the fence used to be.
A sharply starched sunbonnet shadows her face.
She bows her head and leans into a spade,
turning the earth for a new row of beans,
layered in time, anchored to place.

The last light fades
and the stars come out.

The Great Uncle

In 1917 my mother's Uncle George left the farm
for the trenches of France.
When he came home, he went into the house
and didn't come out for three years.

He mended furniture, stoked the fire,
built cabinets, helped my mother.
He was the bachelor uncle
who worked willingly
in the house.

One sharp April day
when it hurt your eyes to look at the sky
and daffodils pushed above the ground,
when sunlight came through the kitchen door,
he went to the barn
and fed the calves.

We never talked about his ways.
He tended the fire and hoped for spring.

The North Field

If I could not see,
I would still know the field
to the north of the barn
by the sound of the corn
and its silky leaves.
I would hear the green blades,
full of moisture and promise,
rich in the warmth of the summer air.
And I would know when the season turned,
when time had had its way with life and green
and silky whispers changed to
clacks, a raking against the others,
curling into our dry brown harvest,
when the kernels are gold
and nights crackle with frost.

War

In 1942 my grandparents took the train
from Indianapolis to Savannah
to see my dad before he shipped out
to California and that peaceful sea
where death swam alongside ships
from Pearl Harbor to Tokyo Bay.
By the time the train crossed the Ohio,
my grandfather, so the story goes,
knew everybody in their car,
exchanged stories of soldier sons
and how crops were doing with so much rain.

Pearl Harbor

All those bodies under the water.
What meaning could rise from
their drowned lives?

Dad knew.
For him it was clear.
Duty.
Country.
Freedom.

He came home,
lived and believed
for those in the harbor
and gave money
for their memorial.

Earth and Air

In another day, an older time
Dad, a young man, would have picked up
and run, leaving behind a rock-strewn farm.
He'd have hopped a freight, gone out west,
worked on the railroad or maybe a ranch.
He'd have ridden the range
on a rough quarter horse,
looking far off,
over the rise
and on.

In a newer time
Mother would have run for office,
starting as mayor of some small town,
moving on to a bid for Congress
and later even a cabinet post.
She'd have loved stomping her foot for justice,
protecting old people and children.

He was tethered and longed for the road,
she dug in and stubborn.
Their Earth and Air made clouds of dust,
invasive with grit.

It was not another time.

In the Dark

One spring I asked Dad why our mama dog, Belle,
had her puppies under the porch
where we couldn't get to them.
He said mummy pups were open to attack
when they were birthing or pooping
so they're careful where they pick their spot.

When Mother became pregnant with me,
Grandmother installed indoor plumbing,
said Mother shouldn't have to go to the outhouse
on the edge of the orchard after dark.
No more misery holding it.
No more trips, huddled in a robe,
bare feet stuffed into old rubber boots.

Where do you go?

Once there was a little girl who lived
in a farmhouse with nowhere to go.

She grew among titans, taught she was light,
a miniature warrior, battling puzzlement
and alcohol drunk through long brooding evenings.

Where do you go when your light leaches out?

Somewhere with snow, heavy and packed,
edged in shadows,
starshine so sharp it leaves knives on the ground,
a cold place with sound frozen in air,
where storms sink into stillness
and no wind blows.

Wagon Train

On her sixth birthday she wanders out
past fields stripped of last year's corn,
past soft breath of cattle around
the old barn,
past a sighing pine
and into the woods

> *thick air moves among cold bare branches*
> *end of winter, not yet spring*

to a downed maple.
She climbs on the tree,
now her mind's covered wagon,
and sits, a small determined driver,
ready to leave with the wagon train.

> *the first green thistles frame*
> *a single bloom of dandelion, a yellow sun*
> *on the thawing ground*

The wagon master rides beside her,
up ahead the daring scout.
The bumbling cook packs up his pots.
They follow the sun into unknown lands.

> *a robin hops along a limb,*
> *warmth coaxes tight buds to burst,*
> *fat under the new born light*

She's wrapped tightly as buds
on the trees, a child alone,
dreaming west.

First Day

The summer before first grade Mother took me shopping for school supplies. A new sweater, a blue satchel to carry my books, a new pair of Buster Brown shoes. Last we went to the hardware store where I picked out a lunch box. Lunch. Box. Those two words can never convey its beauty. The box was covered in shiny stars and on the side "School Daze" blazed in big red letters. I loved the way the lid fit the frame and best of all the latch with its confident click. For the rest of the summer I stored special things in that box—barrettes, a bracelet, a quarter my great uncle gave me for my birthday—all safe under shiny stars.

On my first day of school, Mother gently emptied my lunch box and put in—my lunch. A peanut butter sandwich, chips and an apple. I knew at once: I didn't want food in my beautiful box. And I was very sure I didn't want to take it out of the house. In my room it was shielded from scratches and dents but now I feared for those big red letters, those bright shiny stars. Maybe some kids would kick it on the bus or break it open on the playground. How could it survive the rough life of school?

My heart pounded and my stomach shook. I stood in front of our farmhouse fence in the slanted rays of a September sun, new shoes damp in the dewy grass. Clutching my blue satchel in one hand and my lunch box in the other, I waited for the yellow bus to pick me up and take me to first grade.

Sleeping Warm on the Farm

First day of winter and
dusk winds down into darkness,
falling toward the longest night.
Across the south field
the sun's a red rim,
its distant fire a pretense of warmth.
Derelict cornstalks lie silvered in frost.
In the smokehouse
the beagle curls up with a bundle of cats.
We go to bed early to save on the heat.

Reading Charlotte Bronte

The winter I turned eleven, snow piled up to our windows.
There was no possibility of taking a walk that day.

Bored, I opened an old leather book
and met the girl I was named for.

I read all that day and after lights out, hid under blankets
and read by flashlight,
soaked in her trials, her orphaned state, a scrawny girl with a
spine of oak.

Another Jane, small and thin, this one raised in the cold
house of meanness,
no farm, no safety, no place to belong,
awake by her friend who died in the night,
a throwaway child in a school without heat.

Blue flames danced in the stove in my room.

The Suffering. The Bravery.
        Who was this   *strange, almost unearthly thing?*

Without doubt I knew her
            poor, obscure, plain and little
        a free human being with an independent will.
but puzzled. Why not stay? Why was love wrong?

But this scrap of a woman in her *grey Quaker dress* trudged
away,

every step jarring her broken heart.
> *I need not sell my soul to buy bliss.*

Tucked up in the farm house, snow out my window,
I trailed across England behind my new Cinderella.

Love found.   Love lost.   Love regained at a cost.

It is in vain to say human beings ought to be satisfied with tranquility:
> *they must have action; and they will make it if they cannot find it.*

Jane.
A name to live into.
I was eleven and read through the night.

Scent

around the beginning of May
when school was out
and weather turned soft
Dad took down storm windows
he'd covered in plastic
to keep the worst of winter winds out
and hung up screens
hooked to the sills
in frames six feet tall

the walls of my room
disappeared
and I smelled
freshly cut grass
newly turned earth
the old lilac bush

in one breath
the scents of spring
drifted in

In Summer

tiger lilies
bloomed by the kitchen door,
great orange, spotted blooms
on tall green stalks.
Litters of wild tumbling kittens
practiced their games
upon the lilies
until, torn and bedraggled,
the lilies lay flat,
beauty shredded for a summer,
a year.
In a new summer's heat
more lilies grew,
dressed in fierce orange
and strong black spots,
holding their place
in the cycle of things.

October Primitive

When fields of frost sparkled under the harvest moon,
we put on mittens and thick wool hats,
circled bonfires, warmed our faces,
roasted hot dogs, chased our shadows,
kicked through piles of raked up leaves,
curled and crackling around our feet.
The air tasted of snow.

Red Hats

i.
In winter
Mother dressed me in woolens,
rubber boots and a little red hat.
I wandered past the chicken yard
and out through the orchard,
away from the smokehouse and into fields
where flat frozen corn shucks formed a path.
The woods were grey mist against a snow-filled sky.
Fifty black Angus stayed near the barn.
Cats and dogs trailed after me.
Heavy clouds and bare-branched trees
bent before southwest winds.
Back in the woods I climbed on a hay rake
and pretended I was a pioneer, heading west
in a wagon train.
Mother watched from the kitchen,
so she'd know where I was.
I just followed the bobbing red hat.

ii.
I need help.
I left my mother on this bench
and she's wandered off.
I told her to stay put
but she gets an idea in her head
and then she's gone.
She's a little thing
in a beige winter coat.
She wears glasses
and carries a cane.
And she's wearing a wooly red hat.

Reading Emily Dickinson

At sixteen, I pondered the Recluse.
I'm Nobody! Are you--Nobody--Too?
Through that thick spring season,
backlit with melancholy and milky light,
I wandered in poetic bliss--
at one with dashes--
and intensity.

A Light exists in Spring
Not present on the Year...
When March is scarcely here.

I spent afternoons in my room
alone,
soaking in
A little Madness . . . is wholesome,
loved her dialogues with Death,

Because I could not stop for Death--
He kindly stopped for me--

how she transformed garden
into cloister,

If I can stop one Heart from breaking,

loved my longing
and manipulative pathos
tossed out to a world
that would never understand.

*This is my letter to the World
That never wrote to Me--*

One dreamy spring--

*"Hope" is the thing with feathers--
Judge tenderly--of Me.*

Four Moons

winter

A fox lifts his snout to the scent of blood,
his full moon shadow etched on old snow.
The temperature drops to five below.

spring

Thin sunlight and cold moonbeams fall
from an equinox sky, turning frost to mud, thick and black.
Clods stick to our boots as we clump to the barn.

summer

Grandmother loved her climbing roses, but
never brought them into the house.
When she was dying,
Granddad cut a single white rose,
put it in a vase by her bed.
She thanked him and slowly turned away.

autumn

No rain since May.
The harvest is dust and plowed-under crops.
September's moon rises on ruined fields
and covers next year's hopes with light.

Reading Doctor Zhivago

I write for you.
Your imagination is the stage where my poem plays.
I believe you will pluck my poem in a bottle
from the oceans of the world
and read.

My stories began with Dick and Jane.
I read Cinderella and sanitized Grimm.
The ladies of Cranford thrived in adversity.
Nancy and Sherlock nabbed the bad guys.
The frost was on Orphant Annie's punkin
and Jane married Mr. Rochester.

My glass slippers glittered
in the moonlight of spring.
At the masked ball of enchantment
I waltzed toward my own ever after.

> *The princess has grown old in her palace.*
> *She sits alone in a high stone tower,*
> *a book abandoned in her lap.*

> *Her fairy godmother returns,*
> *waving a wand over unforeseen gifts.*

Time spread out, flat, shining
silver, sunshine
on shallow water,
a blossom drifting
to the ground.

Passion folded into memory,
hunger no hotter than
a distant star.

Attention turned toward Orion
rising, the sorrow of children
and fragile bones.

Now it's winter and snow swirls in darkness.
I know stories of wandering without an arrival,
Heathcliff and Yuri on a streetcar named loss.
Tess and Ophelia in unfinished dramas,
requiems sounding, illicit as love.

I have lived long enough to read *Doctor Zhivago*
where ever afters belong to memories stolen
between hours after midnight
and a slow cloudy dawn.

Histories

i.

When Rupert, our hired man, came from the fields at noon, he washed off his morning's work at the spigot and sat down in the kitchen to Grandmother's feast. Fried chicken, white gravy, mashed potatoes, green beans, yeast rolls, strong tea, apple sauce and yellow cake. As a girl Grandmother had done the plowing in spring. Rupert got the best.

Histories

ii.

When we were six, Johnny McMichael and I got engaged. Our mothers got their hair done in the same beauty shop. It seemed meant to be and lasted until we were seven. In 1966 Johnny turned eighteen, graduated from high school and went to war. He served two tours and saw his best friend blown up. Johnny came home. He was blown up inside. The blown up parts rattled around in him like BBs in a washtub. The world held nothing but noxious dreams and technicolor memory. Slowly he returned to his true world of crops, fields and harvests, a mostly predictable world where his mom had her hair done every week and basketball happened on Friday nights. He was embedded in people who believed in duty and country, who'd known him all his life and believed he'd done the right thing.

Histories

iii.

Sarah Ann and I grew up in the same church, spent Sunday nights in the same youth group, sang in the same high school chorus and marched in the same high school band. We liked the same boy, picked strawberries on June afternoons and sold magazine subscriptions in the fall to fund our class trip. We tried hard in school and longed for romance. We were good girls, never troubled the waters. It's cold now we're not the same.

Histories

iv.
One day when the tenant's boy was around ten, his horse got away from him and ran them both into a fence near the barn. The barbed wire sliced off a finger from the boy's left hand. Everybody was grateful that at least it was his left hand. He played basketball and went on to become a lawyer. He was a smart boy.

The tenant's girl got married right out of high school and moved to a farm just down the road. She had an only daughter and one Sunday night when the daughter was about twenty, the daughter's ex-boyfriend came to the house with a deer rifle and shot the daughter, the tenant's girl and her husband. Finally shot himself. Three closed coffins, all in one room at the funeral home. Nobody knew where the fourth coffin was.

Histories

v.

The November of my sixth grade, the Dixon kids showed up at school. Their dad dragged them up from Kentucky so they could live on the township.

The Dixon in my class was Beatrice. Her eyes were dark and sulky under greasy bangs. She wore skimpy cotton dresses and a tattered old coat, women's shoes that slid around on her feet and no socks. Her bare legs turned blue in our Indiana cold. Beatrice also had lice. For months she wore a grimy bandana that barely covered the bald spot on the back of her head where her hair had been shaved.

One day it was my turn to choose for kickball. I heard my own voice call "Beatrice!" Silence. Complete. No one, not Beatrice, not I, not the other kids believed her name on my lips. I had to say it again before it sunk in. After that I chose my best friend but the strange deed was done. As we ran out to the playground, Beatrice hurried up to me, threw her arm around my shoulder, gave me a big smile (also lice) and said, "Jane, I like you." Stunned, I muttered "I like you, too." in terror that now I might actually have to be her friend, walk with her to music class or, worst of all, sit with her at lunch.

Come spring the Dixons disappeared. Back to Kentucky or some other township. We never saw them again.

Histories

vi.
My cousin Elaine was the prettiest girl in the family. Tall, slender with curly black hair. She'd go to the movies and before the show was over, she'd know every boy in the theater. Girls at school called her "boy crazy" but she knew they were jealous. She was the girl all the boys wanted to date.

Elaine's folks sent her to college but she flunked out her freshman year. When she came home, her hair hung lank and her face was blotchy. She wouldn't go to the movies with us and if she met an old boyfriend, she'd look away. Elaine moved to Indianapolis and got a typing job. The family didn't see her for years. One day she called our grandmother and said she needed to come home to get on her feet. She got off the Greyhound with a wad of medical bills and a little girl.

A few weeks before she died, Elaine told me her doctor said she'd gotten cancer because she'd slept with so many guys. She said she wished she'd cared more about school but she'd ended up in a crowd that partied hard and a lot. Said she thought the guys liked her but she knew now wolves run in packs.

Elaine died the Christmas she turned 31. The family wanted to keep the little girl but the father showed up and took her away.

Histories

vii.

After high school Larry Carter went to the army and then Vietnam. One morning on patrol the kid in front stepped on a mine and the streamy world turned to mud and pain. Larry lost his foot. The kid in front was never found. Larry came home with a new right foot and a bonus of nightmares to fill the gap. In his sleep Viet Cong poured out of hidden tunnels, every soldier waving death in a boot. He tried to wash the nightmares away with plenty of six packs and cigarettes because everyone knew counseling's for crazies. *Our boy isn't crazy. These things take time. He just needs to get back on his feet.*

The Portal

Two young bodies lay in the road,
clothed in a pretense of jungle greens,
covered in twisted metal and dirt.
Indiana boys. They'd been thinking of home,
cars, the girl who wrote,
the one who didn't, an old spotted dog
raised from a pup. Thinking young thoughts
before they stepped on the road.
Souls, cocooned in quiet,
unwrapped from time drifted with the smoke of shells
toward thick dark leaves of the banyan tree,
bootless feet marching the last parade,
laid down invisible rifles,
dropped fading helmets and hand grenades.
The Portal opened among the leaves,
a green invitation in the heavy wet heat.
Two souls, naked and shining,
stepped through the door.

Return

He should have died in the pasture or near the garden, the clover ground his catafalque. Or in the barn as he fed the calves. Not in a metal bed in a sterile room while his roommate watched boxing on a blaring TV. Not in a sealed place where he couldn't hear the last howl of winter or feel the first warmth of spring. He was a man of fields and Angus, woods and seasons. He loved tractors, freshly cut grass and knowing what he'd see when he looked out his door. He should have died where he lived, on ground that was home.

Histories

viii.
The August after John Curran died, hot winds blew across the fields, turned the grass brown and crunchy underfoot. Crops lay stunted, corn half a healthy height and when the winds blew, the stalks crackled as in October.

One blazing afternoon Mother walked out to the barn. Hot wind skinned her hair back and heat shimmered off her cane. She stumbled a step as she leaned over and picked up a little stone from the sun-scorched grass. Full light struck her face. Tired. Tough. Alone. As though she might fall against the wind and die where nothing grew. Slowly she straightened and tossed the useless stone away.

Rain fell that autumn and broke the drought, but it came too late to save the crops. They were long plowed under and gone.

At Ninety-one

Mother shares house with dementia,
rooms where time curls, stretches, stops.

Ancient faces gaze back at her,
their darling girl.
They visit.
They go.

In her house the linear curves back to its origin.
A moment bursts into dream.
I can't remember who's dead,
she says.

Yesterday forever is now.

Season of Dreams

        Mother is busy with visits from the dead.

I dreamed about Pop,
eyes the same bright blue as the sky.
The horses came right up to him.

Mother. I hadn't heard,
was worried she was upset with me
or she didn't know where I was if they needed help
but we had a good visit. Everyone's fine.

Midge, our old beagle dog.
I called her and she looked back
but kept running, nose to the ground
all the way into the woods.

        Mother smiles and shuts her eyes.

by the South Field

One July morning
I drove away from the farmhouse,
away from the barn, the acres and trees.

When I slowed to turn at the corner,
I felt a warm breeze on my face,
heard silky whispers
rustle through crops,
sacred sounds,
born of seed into humid light.
I heard corn growing
in the south field.

Reading Thomas Wolfe

summer before college
with days on the farm
sprawled out
across hay fields
and heat,
languorous
dripping with time

and an old book
taken idly down
from the case
in the front room

Eugene Gant and
his ruined family
violent, voracious

through long days
and warm nights
I read about wildness
coming of age
with death the constant
ticking theme

my bedroom with its yellow walls
and open windows
crickets and night sounds
a moth captured
by the bedside light
smells rolling in
cut grass and dusty corn
filled with words
written by a man from his
need to be known and I read,
waiting for my life to begin,
wanting to leave
this liminal place
and there was Wolfe,
desperate
to get home.

Once a Place

In January the sky turns black, a stage for stars,
their light sharp across the woods.
Eons of starshine touch my breath,
freezing my sighs into bright needles.

I was born between the Ides of March
and the first rising day of spring,
born to daffodils, blown and sturdy,
coated in sunshine, shaking loose seasons,
born, too, with a dust of snow on my shoulders
and winter's chill at my back.

When fields steam in moist heat
and sunflowers loom on impossible stalks,
when light pours across western fields
and the sun rides high above the horizon,
in the east a red moon climbs the August sky,
an indigo sky so thick and close I reach up
and touch both lights.
My hands glitter with crimson dust.

At the back of the farm a hawk soared, its hoarse cry born
from the dying year. As this soul in
flight flowed across cooling earth, I saw the ground rise,
ripple, a loosening of limits until
hawk, land and I were one.

Acknowledgements

"Reading Thomas Wolfe." Magic Again: Selected Poems on Thomas Wolfe: The Thomas Wolfe Society 36 (2015) 39.

"The Great Uncle," "Reading Emily Dickinson," "October Primitive," "The Return," "Season of Dreams." County Lines: A Literary Journal 2 (2015): 2, 50, 66, 75, 102.

Jane Mary Curran lives in Asheville, North Carolina. She is retired from all kinds of wonderful work, including a college professorship in piano and a second career as chaplain with hospice. Now in her third third of life she returns to an old love and savors the joy of words, pen and paper. Her poetry has been published in numerous print and digital journals. She was the winner of both the Summer 2015 Great Smokies Writers Editor's Choice and the Spring 2016 Great Smokies Writers Editor's Choice Competitions in poetry. She's the author of *Midwives of the Spirit—Thoughts on Caregiving*.

www.ingramcontent.com/pod-product-compliance
Lightning Source LLC
Chambersburg PA
CBHW060505080526
44584CB00015B/1559